CRETE

**Jack Altman
Catherine Gerber**

JPMGUIDES

Mediterranean climate

CONTENTS

3	**This Way Crete**
7	**Flashback**
13	**On the Scene**
13	The Centre
27	The East
33	The West
49	**Shopping**
53	**Dining Out**
57	**Sports**
58	**The Hard Facts**
64	**Index**

Features
16 Nikos Kazantzakis
43 Trekking in Crete
46 The Backdrop

Maps
61 Agios Nikolaos
62 Rethimnon
63 Chania

Fold-out map
Crete
Iraklion
Palace of Knossos

enduring traditions

dreamy beaches

archaeological sites

THIS WAY CRETE

Fiercely independent-minded, the people of Crete think of their island as a place apart from the rest of Greece. Inhabiting by far the biggest of all the Greek islands, the proudest Cretans even refer to their home as a "continent". And indeed, Crete does offer just about everything one might find on a whole continent: spectacular craggy mountains and pretty green meadows, great beaches, good food and, not least, the cultural treasures of the Minoans, Europe's oldest civilisation.

Nature and Mythology

Crete owes its ancient development to its position as a trade bridge between three actual continents: Europe, Asia and Africa. The proximity of Africa is also reflected in the subtropical flora you will spot on walks in the island's interior—after all, Crete lies further south than Tangiers, Algiers and Tunis. In Greek mythology, Crete occupies an especially prominent role. This is the island where Zeus was born and where he, disguised as a bull, swam ashore with the abducted Levantine princess Europa on his back. On Crete she bore him three sons, including Minos, the first king of Knossos. The palace of Knossos, Crete's main tourist attraction, is associated with the myth of the bull-man Minotaur.

Where to Go

Midway along the north coast, Iraklion (also spelled Heraklion or Herakleion) is the island's capital and commercial centre. It has lively cultural, culinary and shopping scenes as well as a stunning collection of ancient treasures, mostly Minoan, in its newly revamped Archaeological Museum. A visit here should not be missed, either before or after a tour of the nearby palace of Knossos.

Iraklion is also a good base for excursions to other major archaeological sites, such as Phaistos, Agia Triada and Gortyn, and to the southern beach towns of Matala and Agia Galini.

The coast immediately to the east of Iraklion is the heart of Crete's package tourism industry and jammed with hotels and resorts, especially in Chersonissos and Malia. Things get a lot quieter the farther east you go. Agios Nikolaos and Elounda are sophisticated seaside resorts on scenic Mirabello Bay, while Sitia has a more laid-back, modest vibe. All are good gateways to the mountain villages, the windmill-dotted Lassithi Plateau with the cave where Zeus was born, the lovely palm beach at Vaï and the Minoan palace ruins of Malia and Kato Zakros. On the south coast, unassuming Ierapetra is the centre of Crete's greenhouse industry and a launch pad for excursions to unpopulated Chrissi Island.

West of Iraklion are the charming towns of Rethimnon and Chania, whose architecture and character were greatly influenced by the Venetians and the Ottomans. Both are picturesque bases for exploring the Amari Valley, Zeus's childhood home on Mount Ida (now called Psiloritis) and the celebrated gorges of Samaria and Imbros in the Lefka Ori range. Both of these canyons spill out at uncrowded pebble coves and beaches fringing the Libyan Sea. The attractive south coast fishing villages—Paleochora, Sougia, Loutro and Chora Sfakion—are wonderful destinations for individualists.

In the far northwest, Kastelli Kissamou is a relaxed resort with easy access to the remote and stunning Balos Lagoon and the pink-hued sands of Elafonissi, a protected nature reserve.

Crete's mythical mountains. Zeus' father Cronus had the nasty habit of devouring his newborns out of fear of being overthrown, as had been prophesied by an oracle. To spare her latest child such a fate, his wife Rhea gave birth in a remote cave tucked into Crete's Dikti Mountains. She then presented Cronus with a rock wrapped in swaddling cloth, which he promptly swallowed. Zeus, meanwhile, grew into the "father of all gods", being fed goat's milk and honey in another Cretan cave on Mount Ida. Both caves are open to visitors.

Huber/Huber

A Geography Lesson

Shaped like a lazy swimmer floating belly up in the Mediterranean, Crete is 250 km (156 miles) long and 60 km (37 miles) at its widest point. Some 600,000 people call the island home, with the majority concentrated along the north coast, which is also where most of the resorts are located. The rugged mountainous interior divides into three ranges—the Lefka Ori (White Mountains) to the west, the tall peaks of Mount Psiloritis in the centre, and the Dikti range in the east. In between are fertile valleys, lofty plateaus, caves and rugged gorges, including the Samaria Gorge, one of the longest in Europe.

In springtime, the countryside is redolent with orchids, crocuses, sage and other wildflowers, to be replaced with yellow carpets of buttercups later in the season. Silvery groves of olives abound, along with orchards of lemons, oranges, apricots, almonds and figs cultivated for the city markets.

The Cretan People

The distinctive personality of the islanders—proud, tough and resilient on the surface, but deep down warm and generous—is the natural result of their long and often arduous history. To their taste for the good life, instilled by their Minoan beginnings, has been added a tenacious instinct for survival. Through several waves of invaders—Romans, Venetians, Turks—the Cretans ultimately prevailed through their strong faith, a fascinating blend of austere Greek Orthodox Christianity and enduring ancient superstition. One of the most gratifying experiences for a visitor is to break through that stoical crust to the cordial smile and hearty embrace of friendship. It is the reward of mutual respect.

The Cretans like to relax around a refreshing glass of *raki*. Join them with a smile and a *Yamas* (Cheers!).

Sir Arthur Evans interpreted the Minoan symbol as the horns of the sacrificial bull, the "horns of consecration".

FLASHBACK

Crete has long played leading roles in mythology and history. Europe's first advanced civilisation, the Minoans, was named after Zeus' son: the legendary King Minos. The Minoans dominated the island from 2700 BC to 1500 BC. The vacuum created by their disappearance was quickly filled by a succession of marauders—Mycenaeans, Dorians, Romans, Arabs, Venetians and Turks—before unity with Greece was finally achieved in 1913.

The Minos Touch

Named by archaeologists after the legendary King Minos, son of Zeus and Europa, the splendid Minoan society emerged around 3000 BC and ended rather abruptly—possibly on account of a cataclysmic volcanic eruption on nearby Santorini island—around 1450 BC. The origin of the Minoans is not yet fully understood. The latest study, published in 2013, suggests that they were descendents of Neolithic populations who migrated to Europe from the Middle East and Turkey and then moved south to settle on Crete.

Minoan society reached its cultural peak around 2000 BC, when all the major palaces at Knossos, Phaistos, Malia and Kato Zakros were built and the island's population reached some 2 million, more than triple today's number. The architecture and layout of the palaces reflect a highly sophisticated civilisation. Compounds have multiple stories, plumbing and drainage as well as separate areas for workshops, storage, living, worshipping and ruling. There are no defensive ramparts, but plenty of roof gardens, bathing pools, banquet halls and spacious bedrooms.

The level of craftsmanship and artistry was extraordinarily advanced as well. Rooms and shrines were sheathed in frescoes and decorated with elaborate figurines such as the snake goddess or the bull-leaper. Goldsmiths fashioned exquisitely detailed jewellery from imported gold, silver, ivory, bronze and precious gems. The other major accomplishment was the emergence of a written language, called Linear A, which to this day remains undeciphered.

Crete's fleet was among the largest in the Mediterranean and used primarily for trading rather than military purposes. Remnants of its exports that included honey, olive oil, wine as well as timber, jewellery, pottery, cloth, wool and herbs, have been found throughout the Mediterranean.

The demise of the Minoans is also shrouded in mystery: indeed, a massive eruption of a volcano on Santorini occurred around 1450 BC. This may have caused a tsunami that wiped out coastal communities, led to fires that destroyed the palaces (except Knossos) and villages, and resulted in extensive ash fall that killed off crops, causing a grand-scale food shortage. Although these events may not have wiped out the Minoans completely, they seem to have weakened them sufficiently to allow the Mycenaeans from mainland Greece to conquer and occupy the island. The main contribution of the invaders is the introduction of Linear B, a written language adapted from Linear A and considered an early form of modern Greek.

The Mycenaeans' luck ran out in the 12th century BC when they in turn were conquered by the Dorians sweeping down from the Balkans.

Rome and Byzantium

Crete remained a silent backwater throughout Classical Greek history, providing only a few professional soldiers for the armies of Alexander the Great. In 67 BC, it became a province of the Roman Empire with Gortyn in southern Crete as its capital. Over the next 450 years, the Roman contribution was above all practical and material—new roads and aqueducts and extensive plumbing.

Christianity was brought to Crete by St Paul himself, around AD 60, who shortly thereafter appointed Titus as the island's first bishop. Nevertheless, the new faith was slow in catching on in Crete. After the Roman Empire was divided into an Eastern and a Western section at the end of the fourth century, Crete found itself part of the eastern side under Byzantium, which imposed a highly structured and hierarchical society. Gradually the Cretans were won over to the Orthodox Church.

This new cohesiveness was first tested by an Arab invasion of 824. The new conquerors set up their capital on the north coast at Rabd el-Khandak (today's Iraklion) and used Crete primarily as a base for piracy. After a series of failed attempts to recapture the island, Byzantine general Nikiforas Fokas finally succeeded in 961. The last recalcitrant Arabs were persuaded to surrender when they learned that all their comrades outside the fortress were being systematically decapitated by their Byzantine captors.

Venetian Crete
In the early 13th century, Crete was up for grabs again when Byzantium lost out to the Fourth Crusaders. In subsequent horse-trading, Piedmontese prince Boniface of Montferrat sold the island to Venice for a straight 10,000 silver marks in 1204. For the next four and a half centuries, the Venetians made Crete the the linchpin of their commercial empire. Fortifications at their ports of Iraklion, Rethimnon and Chania still bear the glorious emblem of the Lion of St Mark. Their architecture was the most attractive on the island since the disappearance of the Minoans.

Under the Venetians, local Cretans were exposed to Renaissance culture, resulting in high levels of cultural and artistic achievement in the 16th and 17th centuries. A key work of vernacular poetry from this period was Erotokritos by Vitsentzos Kornaros. In painting, post-Byzantine art found expression in the Cretan School of icon painting with two Iraklion-born artists as its key players. Michail Damaskinos (ca. 1530–1593) softened traditional Byzantine austerity with a rich use of colour learned in Venice to create masterful icons for the Orthodox Church. Even more celebrated was Domenikos Theotokopoulos (1541–1614), painter, sculptor and architect. He began his career by painting icons but converted to Catholicism and, after travelling to Venice, Rome, and then Toledo in Spain, became known to the world as El Greco. In the fierce intensity of his painting, he remained faithful to his Cretan origins, often adding "the Cretan" to his signature.

Byzantine church in Fodele, the village where El Greco is believed to have been born.

Turkish Takeover

Starting in the 16th century, Crete became a major stake in the struggle between Christian Europe and the Islamic Ottoman Empire. Extending their power across the western Mediterranean, the Turks attacked the island in the 1530s with pirate raids on Chania and Sitia, launched from Algeria by the formidable Khair ad-Din, known as Barbarossa. The Venetians fended them off and built new fortifications which resisted full-scale invasion for more than a century until first Chania yielded in 1645, then Rethimnon in the following year.

The last bastion, the capital Candia (Iraklion), was besieged for 21 years. Venetian and Cretan forces humiliated successive Turkish commanders, even causing one of them to be punished back in Constantinople with public strangulation. After the city was finally captured with the negotiated peaceful departure of the Venetians in 1669, it was calculated that 118,000 Turks had died in the prolonged struggle, compared with the Christians' losses of over 30,000.

For more than two centuries—until 1898—Crete was part of the Ottoman Empire and stuck in a state of obscurity and inertia. Life under the Venetians had often been tough, but at least it had given free rein to the islanders' creativity. Turkish governors did little more than collect taxes and stifle all cultural life. Rather than build mosques, they replaced church steeples with minarets.

From time to time, Cretan rebels hiding in the mountainous interior rose in rebellion. One of the most famous revolts was led in 1770 in Sfakia by a wealthy shipowner named Daskalogiannis. Under the slogan "Freedom or Death", the cycle of violent rebellion and bloody reprisals continued well into the 19th century. During the Cretan Revolt of 1866, in one especially tragic act of defiance, the abbot and villagers holed up in Moni Arkadiou blew up the monastery, killing everyone inside, rather than surrender to the Turks.

In the end, it took the intervention of the Great Powers (Britain, France, Italy and Russia) to rid Crete of Turkish control in 1898 and to turn it into an independent state helmed by Prince George of Greece.

Greek at Last

It was the later Greek prime minister, Cretan-born Eleftherios Venizelos (1864–1936), who became the leader in the Enosis movement to unite Crete with Greece (from Greek *henosis*, union). In 1905 he created a "Revolutionary Assembly" in the village of Theriso, near Chania, demanding reforms and political union. He quickly gathered enough support in the official Cretan Assembly that its members declared unilateral union with Greece in 1908. It would take another five years before the act was officially recognised by Greece.

In the 1920s, it also fell to Venizelous, by now prime minister of Greece, to oversee the great population exchange between Greek Orthodox citizens of Turkey and the Muslim citizens of Greece that had been agreed to by the 1923 Treaty of Lausanne. Crete saw the last 10,000 Turks depart, while 13,000 Greek refugees arrived from Turkey.

Throughout this tumultuous period, British archaeologist Sir Arthur Evans (1851–1941) was digging into a hillside to uncover the fabled palace of King Minos at Knossos. This unexpected discovery of a lost civilisation, coupled with a growing appreciation of Crete's natural beauty, launched the new industry of tourism. The island's economy also benefited from the modernisation of its agriculture.

Minoan architecture has inspired a modern luxury resort.

War and Peace

World War II brought yet another invasion. The lightning German advance through the Balkans drove the forces of Britain and its Commonwealth allies to retreat across the Greek mainland down to Crete. Backed by the Cretan militia, the effort to resist German capture of the island cost the Allies 2,000 dead and 12,000 prisoners. Remaining troops were evacuated, leaving the islanders to harass the Germans throughout the war with their time-honoured technique of guerrilla warfare. Villagers were routinely shot and villages razed in reprisal. In addition, the bombs and shells destroyed a large part of the island's towns, and subsequent rebuilding was often carried out with more haste than taste.

Today, more care is being taken with new construction in the coastal resorts. The island's natural charm and the great cultural traditions of its ancient civilisation are treated with the respect they deserve. The Minoan taste for the fine things of life has not been lost.

Walk out to the fortress to see the Lion of St Mark sculpted on its walls.

ON THE SCENE

You can chop Crete neatly up into three parts—the East, the Centre and the West. The main resorts at the eastern end of the island are Agios Nikolaos, Elounda, Sitia and, on the south coast, Ierapetra. In the centre, the charms of the capital of Iraklion lie in its cultural and culinary diversions. To the west, Rethimnon and Chania are Crete's prettiest towns.

The Centre

The heart of Crete is a region of superlatives. You can potter around Iraklion, work on your tan at its longest sandy beaches (Chersonissos and Malia) or get acquainted with the mysterious Minoans, Europe's oldest civilisation. Before visiting their 4000-year-old palace ruins at Knossos, Malia, Phaistos and Agia Triada, stop by Iraklion's excellent Archaeological Museum.

In the primitive Diktaean Cave where Zeus was born, above the village of Psychro, you can embrace the world of mythology. If you're keen on even more caves, head to the old hippie hangout of Matala on the south coast. On your way back, don't forget to sample Crete's increasingly fine wines on a tour through the Iraklion Wine Country south of Knossos.

Iraklion

A population of more than 170,000 makes Iraklion, the island's capital, the fourth largest city in Greece. While it's too busy to be conducive to a beach holiday, it has a great deal to offer in the way of historical and cultural interest. Top of the list is the outstanding Archaeological Museum, which boasts the most important collection of Minoan art in the world. Other draws include handsome vestiges of its Venetian past, including an impressive fort, Byzantine icons in its churches as well as cosmopolitan café, culinary and nightlife scenes.

Archaeological Museum

One of the finest museums of antiquities in the world, Iraklion's archaeological collection comprises 5,500 years worth of finds from the Neolithic to the Roman periods, including the most comprehensive collection of artefacts associated with the Minoan civilisation.

The main museum building, which had been closed for renovation since 2006 (the most important objects were showcased in a smaller annex off Hatzidaki Street), finally reopened its doors in May 2014. The new exhibition occupies a total of 24 rooms.

The **Rooms of Sculptures** present outstanding examples of statues and objects from the Archaic, the Classical, the Hellenistic and the Roman periods. In one of the rooms, statues of gods are juxtaposed with those of statesmen and other mortals. Standouts include a headless statue of Emperor Hadrian and a small marble figure of Pan.

The biggest crowd-pleasers, though, are upstairs in the **Hall of Frescoes** where you can admire the celebrated original Minoan wall paintings from Knossos. The Dolphin Fresco from the Queen's bedroom, the Cup Bearers from the South Prophylaeum, the Griffin Fresco from the Throne Room, the Prince of the Lilies, La Parisienne and many others are all handily assembled in one large gallery.

The museum houses many other key Minoan treasures. These include the famous **Phaistos Disk** whose mysterious spiralling hieroglyphics are believed to represent some kind of religious prayer or hymn and have not yet been deciphered.

The height of Knossos' prosperity, from 1700 to 1400 BC, is epitomised by the black steatite **Bull's Head chalice** that served as a centrepiece for ritual libations.

Also intriguing are the two polychrome faïence **snake goddesses**, also found at Knossos. One grasps a pair of snakes with a baby leopard on her head, while the other goddess has snakes coiled around her waist and headdress.

The merry scenes on the **Harvester Vase** from Agia Triada depict olive harvesters celebrating with song and dance. Also from Agia Triada, found in its necropolis, is a stunning painted **sarcophagus** which provides clues about Minoan funeral rites.

An exquisite example of Minoan jewellery is the intricate golden **Bee Pendant** found at Malia.

Venetian Harbour

Commanding the entrance to the historic harbour, Iraklion's hulking **Fort** was completed in 1540 in the face of the growing menace of Turkish invaders. Called Rocca al Mare by the Venetians and Koules by the Turks, it was the main obstacle to Turkish conquest during the 21-year siege that ended in 1669. The defiant emblem of the Venetian Empire, the Lion of St Mark, is sculpted on the fortress wall facing out to the Sea of Crete. The walk along the jetty past colourful fishing boats is especially nice at sunset, but the structure itself is currently closed.

Also part of the Venetian harbour are the tall quayside arcades of the **Venetian Asenal**, the 16th-century shipyards where the Venetians repaired their ships, getting them ready for another round of trade and warfare in the Mediterranean.

City Walls

The Venetian-built ramparts extend 4 km (2.5 miles) and provide interesting views of the city's historical core. Access is easiest at the **Martinengo Bastion** on the south side. Here, at the highest point in town, you'll also find the grave of Iraklion's famous local son, 20th-century writer Nikos Kazantzakis, author of *Zorba the Greek*.

Agios Titos

The architecture of Iraklion's churches often reflects Crete's chequered history, having gone from Catholic church under the Venetians to a mosque under the Turks and back again to a church, but this time Orthodox, under the Greeks. Such was the fate of the

A faïence figurine of a snake goddess, connected with the protection and welfare of the home.

Church of Agios Titos, which guards the skull of Titus, the island's patron saint. A disciple of the apostle Paul, he brought the Christian message to Crete in AD 59. In order to keep it safe from the occupying Turks, the retreating Venetians had taken the skull with them three centuries ago, and it was only returned to the island in 1966.

Municipal Art Gallery

The former Basilica of Agios Markos (St Mark's Basilica) was

NIKOS KAZANTZAKIS

One of Greece's most important modern writers and philosophers, Nikos Kazantzakis, was born in 1883 in Iraklion, which at the time was still part of the Ottoman Empire. He graduated from law school in Athens in 1906 and then moved to Paris to study journalism and literature. Kazantzakis was a prolific writer who, in his early life, was greatly influenced by Nietzsche and Bergson. His most famous novel is *Zorba the Greek*, published in 1946 and turned into an Academy Award-winning movie in 1964 with Anthony Quinn in the title role.

Kazantzakis' fascinating life and work are getting the full treatment at the **Kazantzakis Museum** in Myrtia, a mere 15 km (9 miles) southeast of Iraklion. Here you can watch an engaging documentary, learn about his philosophy, examine personal possessions and get a thorough overview of his works, which also included the controversial *Last Temptation of Christ*.

The **Historical Museum of Crete** in Iraklion also dedicates a section to the city's famous son. A highlight is the recreation of his study in Antibes, France, where the author spent his last years (1948–1957). Nearby, in the Martinengo Bastion, you can pay your respects at **Kazantzakis's grave**. The moving inscription on his tombstone sums up his philosophy: "I hope for nothing. I fear nothing. I am free."

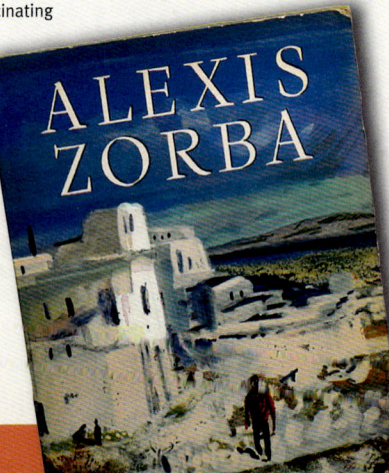

flickr.com/Orloff

built in 1239, converted to a mosque after the 16th-century Turkish invasion and restored to its present form in the 1960s. No longer a church, it houses the Municipal Art Gallery whose changing exhibits often showcase Cretan artistic talents.

Morosini Fountain
Four lions support the lovely 17th-century Morosini Fountain, which was named after a Venetian governor. It punctuates busy **Plateia Venizelou**, a carfree square dedicated to Cretan-born Prime Minister Eleftherios Venizelos and flanked by cafés and bars that are bustling at all hours.

Agia Ekaterini
Agia Ekaterini (St Catherine's) was once a refuge for Byzantine scholars and icon-painters after the fall of Constantinople in 1453. It now houses a collection of Cretan icons, most famously those by the great post-Byzantine artist Michail Damaskinos. At press time, the exhibit was closed for renovation with no reopening date set.

Historical Museum
Much more engaging than its name might suggest, this museum tells the story of Crete from the 4th to the 20th centuries. Its documents, weapons, photographs, sculptures and other objects reflect the impact of the succession of foreign invaders—Byzantine, Venetian, Turkish and, in the modern era, German.

Upstairs are two rare early paintings by Crete's most renowned artist, Domenikos Theotokopoulos, better known as El Greco. One of them is a fantasized depiction of St Catherine's monastery at the foot of Mount Sinai (1569).

On the second floor is the reconstructed study of author Nikos Kazantzakis, with his desks, books, manuscripts and personal property. Another highlight on the same floor is a comprehensive multimedia exhibit on World War II and the Battle of Crete with special attention given to the Cretan resistance.

Finally, on the third floor, a folklore section showcases aspects of country life with traditional costumes, textiles and kitchen utensils.

Central Market
Municipal markets are always good places in which to feel the town's pulse. Although it has become more tourist-oriented in recent years, Iraklion's market on 1866 Street is no exception. Oriental and local spices and herbs set the olfactory stage, fruit and vegetables add the colour and hunks of meat and glistening fish heighten the drama.

Fodele

Anyone interested in El Greco (1541–1614), who usually signed his paintings with his full name in Greek letters "Domenikos Theotokopoulos, the Cretan", should make a pilgrimage to Fodele, 30 km (18 miles) west of Iraklion. The painter is believed to have been born in this tiny village surrounded by orange and lemon trees. There's a **bust** of the artist in the main square and the small **El Greco House Museum** northwest of the village, with copies of some of his works.

Opposite the museum, the Byzantine **Church of the Panagia** has superb icons and frescoes.

A few kilometres south of Fodele, the monastery of **Agios Pandeleimon**, one of the biggest in Crete, dates from the end of the Venetian era. It has superb icons and frescoes from the 17th to the 19th centuries.

South of Iraklion

On excursions from Iraklion to the archaeological sites and beaches of the central region, the journey itself is a great part of the pleasure. The passage over the mountains takes you through spectacular vistas of fertile farmland, carpeted with colourful wildflowers in springtime. The villages include Zaros, Matala and Agia Galini.

fotolia.com/Fotographik

The Minotaur myth. Sporting a bull's head and a human body, the Minotaur is a central figure in Cretan mythology. After King Minos angered Poseidon, the god took revenge by tricking Minos' wife Pasiphaë into mating with a bull, which produced the bizarre creature. The king imprisoned the monster in a labyrinth and fed him an annual diet of 14 Athenian boys and girls. One of the doomed young men, Theseus, heir to the Athenian throne, was determined to kill the Minotaur but couldn't think of a way to get back out of the labyrinth. Helplessly in love with the brave youth, Ariadne, daughter of Minos, came up with the simple idea of giving Theseus some thread to trace his path in and out. Theseus managed to slew the Minotaur, then left Crete together with Ariadne only to desert her, pregnant, on the island of Naxos.

Knossos

The Minoan palace of Knossos, which was excavated and partly restored by British archaeologist Sir Arthur Evans in the early 20th century, is Crete's number one sightseeing draw. It originated over 3,500 years ago and was the centre of the first highly sophisticated society on European soil. The sprawling grounds are a 20-minute drive or easy bus ride south of Iraklion. Plan to spend at least two hours to do this amazing site justice, preferably in the afternoon when visitor crowds have thinned significantly.

The Complex

With an estimated 1,200 workrooms, storerooms, living spaces, corridors and shrines, Knossos is by far the largest of the Minoan royal palaces. As is typical of all them, they were distributed over several wings up to four stories high and arranged around a large rectangular courtyard.

Past the ticket office, a bougainvillea-flanked path leads to the west court where a bust pays respects to Sir Arthur Evans. En route, you'll pass three round storage pits called Koloures. In front of you is the grand western façade of which only the foundations survive; note the blackened traces of the fire that damaged the palace around 1500 BC. North of here, in the northwest corner of the palace grounds, steps mark the location of an **outdoor theatre** where up to 500 spectators gathered for dances, boxing, wrestling and other sporting events. This was perhaps reserved for commoners rather than the courtiers using the central courtyard.

The palace is entered via the north entrance, a raised and columned structure decorated with a relief fresco of a charging bull. From here it's just a few steps to the heart of the palace, the Central Courtyard.

Central Courtyard

The main inner court is a veritable arena measuring 28 m in width and 53 m in length. The vast courtyard was most likely enclosed on all four sides. Crowned by emblematic bull-horns, vermilion and gold columns supported grandstand-like galleries for spectators gathered for bull-leaping competitions and other ritual tournaments.

West Wing

The west wing of the palace had official functions and contained the palace's shrines, store rooms and administrative rooms. The most important section is the **Throne Room**, a windowless, low-ceilinged chamber entered via an antechamber and decorated with frescoes depicting griffins and plants. To the left, light filters down into a so-called **Lustral Basin** that may have been used for ritual purification.

Past the Throne Room, a staircase leads to the upper floor, where Evans believed the official state and reception rooms to have been located. He dubbed the area **Piano Nobile**, in reference to Italian palazzos that have a similar layout. To the right of the staircase, above the Throne Room, the restored **Fresco Room** contains replicas of Knossos' most famous frescoes (the original fragments are at Iraklion's Archaeological Museum). Walking south through the Piano Nobile you'll spot a series of storage rooms called **West Magazines** before arriving at a staircase leading down to the **South Propylaeum**, a columned portal sporting the wall-sized Cup-Bearer Fresco of men carrying libation vessels.

East Wing

East of the central courtyard is the palace's residential wing, which once consisted of four stories, two overlooking the courtyard and two more built into the hillside beneath. The lower stories were entered via the impressive **Grand Staircase**. Visitors have to take a different route down a ramp. The royal apartments as such are inaccessible but it's possible to sneak a view of the **Queen's Megaron** (bedroom) embellished with the delightful Dolphin Fresco. Her bathroom has a clay bathtub and toilet. Next door, a guard room bearing the insignia of shields and the Minoan double axe precedes the king's chamber, known as the **Hall of the Double Axes**.

Palace Workshops

Stone-masons, potters, tailors and goldsmiths who worked for the royal household had their workshops inside the palace precincts, north of the royal chambers. Also here are the **storehouses** for the royal kitchens. Most spectacular are the giant pithoi, ornate earthenware storage-jars—for grain, oil and wine—with loops for carrying-ropes. You can also detect remnants of the palace's elaborate drainage system.

Gortyn

Olive groves and flowering shrubs provide the setting for the archaeological site of Gortyn (or Gortis, to go by its ancient name), about 46 km (28 miles) southwest of Iraklion. Of minor importance in Minoan times, it became the island capital under the Romans in 67 BC with over a quarter of a million inhabitants and numerous temples, theatres, the governor's palace, public baths and an amphitheatre.

The main section of the site lies within a fenced area to the north of the road. The first key sight you'll spot is the barrel-vaulted 6th-century ruin of the Early Christian **Basilica of Agios Titos**, dedicated to the island's missionary saint and first bishop, a disciple of St Paul.

Nearby is the **Odeon**, a Roman theatre, and on its north side, the Law Code of Gortyn—called **Gortyn Code** or Great Code—inscribed in stone block by Dorian settlers around 500 BC. Decrees relating to property, inheritance, slaves, adultery, divorce and rape are spelled out in some 600 rows of angular letters, to be read alternately from left to right and right to left.

Zaros

At the southern foot of Mt Ida, Zaros is a delightful village famous for its spring water. Just outside town, the enchanting Lake Votomos is the jumping-off point for a moderately strenuous hike through the **Rouvas Gorge**, which ends at the chapel of Agios Ioannis.

While in Zaros, also take the scenic drive west to the frescoed Byzantine church of **Agios Fanourios**, which is all that remains of Valsamonero monastery.

Lendas

Also known by its Phoenician name, Lebena, this pretty little bay lies about 34 km (21 miles)

Replicas of the frescoes showing figures known as the Cup-Bearers in the South Propylaeum.

south of Gortyn over the Asterousia Mountains. It served the Greco-Roman town both as a port and, thanks to its therapeutic spring waters, as a health spa. Excavations have revealed the remains of the Sactuary of Asclepius and the spa's floor mosaic.

Phaistos (Festos)

The superb southern location on a low ridge looking out over the Messara Plain to the Libyan Sea made Phaistos a natural choice for the Minoan kings' winter palace. The ruins reveal a more intimate version of the royal residence at Knossos. A bewitching view greets each stage of your progress, the panoramas clearly incorporated into the architects' plans. Vineyards and olive groves are scattered across the plain watered by the Geropotamos River. It is cooled by light winds from the north where, behind you, the peaks of the Psiloritis mountain range are still capped with snow into late spring.

Before reaching the main precincts down a staircase from the north court, you pass on the right an **open-air theatre**, almost triangular in shape and among the oldest in the world. On your left, a second stairway, more ceremonial in scale, rises to the palace's monumental entrance hall, the **Propylaeum**.

In the north wing, past the **Peristyle Hall**, its column bases still visible, lie the royal chambers. The famous Phaistos Disk (in Iraklion's Archaeological Museum) was found in the servants' quarters further east.

As at Knossos, the sanctuary is accompanied by a double-pillared **crypt**. Stone benches line the walls of the oratory. A large part of the central courtyard has disappeared down the slope, but you can still see the column bases of the portico on the court's western side. From the sanctuary, a long corridor leads away to the **workshops** of the blacksmiths and potters. In the **storehouses** are large earthenware pithoi jars for grain, wine and oil.

Agia Triada

More a villa than palace, Agia Triada lies just 3 km (2 miles) west of Phaistos and was named for a nearby 14th-century Venetian church (though not the Byzantine church of Agios Georgios that overlooks the site). The L-shaped structure may have originally served as a country manor for the Minoan royal court.

Besides the fine view over **Messara Bay**, in ancient times much nearer to the villa, alabaster paving suggests a certain degree of luxury. A five-pillared portico and stairway lead north from the villa to the remains of a village built by Mycenaean Greeks in 1200 BC. Remnants of its shopping arcades can be seen around the town market *(agora)*.

Matala

The beautiful bay of Matala, south of Phaistos, has been popular since the 1960s when hippies (including Joni Mitchell and Bob Dylan) camped out in caves that were used as tombs by the Romans. Since 2011, the Matala Beach Festival revives the hippie spirit. The cliffside caves, which can be explored, overlook the pretty little town whose fine, sandy beach, seaside tavernas and souvenir shops are deluged with day-trippers in summer.

If the beach at Matala gets too crowded, the long sandy strand of **Kommos**, about 2 km (1.5 miles) north of here, is a lovely alternative. A couple of tavernas provide sustenance and there's even a small archaeological site to explore. The beach runs about 2 km north to the laid-back seaside village of **Kalamaki** with shops and a taverna-lined waterfront.

Agia Galini

West of Phaistos, Agia Galini has an attractive location and a huddle of houses built into a steep hillside above a pretty harbour and a small beach. Alas, this erstwhile picturesque fishing village has largely sacrificed its charms to the tourism industry. However, there are some decent fish restaurants, and you can go out in a fishing boat to escape the crowds.

Triopetra and Agios Pavlos

A short drive west of Agia Galini lie two of Crete's most gorgeous south coast beaches that have largely managed to stay off the tourist radar. Both draw their share of yoga and Thai Chi groups.

Soaking up the sun on the rocks of Matala.

First up is **Agios Pavlos**, which consists of a smallish bay with a crescent of grey sand and a couple of tavernas. Quieter and even more beautiful is **Sandhills beach**, reached in a 10-minute walk over the headland and down a steep sand dune. Bring whatever you need with you.

A mostly paved road connects Agios Pavlos with the two beaches of **Triopetra**, named for the three rocks that jut into the Libyan Sea. The main swimming beach is west of the rocks and has coarse sand and great sunsets.

East of Iraklion

The coast east of Iraklion is the hub of Crete's package tourism industry with nearly unbroken development all the way to Malia via Cherssonisos. Worthwhile sightseeing stops include the Minoan Palace at Malia and the Cretaquarium near Gournes.

Cretaquarium

On a former US military base near **Gournes**, about 18.5 km (12 miles) east of Iraklion, the spotlight is on the diversity of Mediterranean marine life at the modern and educational Cretaquarium. Kids especially are enchanted by drifting jellyfish, pulsating anemones, tiny sea horses and fierce sharks. All in all there are 250 species in 90 tanks.

Chersonissos

About 25 km (15.5 miles) east of Iraklion, Chersonissos is the centre of Crete's package tourism industry. Scores of tightly packed, hulking resorts draw sun-hungry visitors from Germany, Scandinavia, Britain and Eastern Europe. The emphasis here is on water sports and hedonistic pleasures—the waterfront is chock-a-block with bars, dance clubs, tavernas with large terraces and even British-style pubs. Diversions away from the resorts include two family-friendly water parks. It's hard to fathom today that Chersonissos was once an important port city under the Greeks and Romans. Down in the harbour are the underwater remains of ancient quays, piers and jetties, while a craggy promontory known as **Kastri** features the ruins of an Early Christian basilica (perhaps 5th century). Roman fish tanks are cut in the rock; freshly caught fish would be kept here until needed.

Malia

Malia is similar in popularity to Cherssonisos but does have the added appeal of a charming Old Town as well as the remains of a **Minoan palace**, discovered in 1915. Built around the same time as Knossos, there is no elaborate reconstruction here, just a picturesque set of ruins that reflects the classic ground plan: a ceremonial staircase, corridors, royal chambers and store rooms are all wrapped around the central courtyard. The famous golden Bee Pendant, now on view at Iraklion's Archaeological Museum, was among the treasures unearthed at this palace.

A major point of interest at the southwest corner of the courtyard is a round limestone slab with 34 indentations around its edge and known as a **Kernos**. Its purpose is not yet well understood, but it might have been a ritual harvest altar for grains and seeds. The most important rooms, including shrines, offices and storerooms, were west of the courtyard.

Next to the **Pillar Crypt**, a justly named **Grand Staircase** once led to the second story of the palace. Behind a raised **Loggia** for sacred ceremonies, stairs descend to a ritual bath similar to the early Christians' baptismal font.

Diktaean Cave

A certain amount of fitness is required to visit the mythological birthplace of Zeus. It's above the village of **Psychro** on the windmill-strewn Lassithi Plateau, about 28 km (17 miles) south of Malia. From the parking lot, it's a steep 1-km (half-mile) walk to the entrance, either via a paved path or a stony trail. From there, slippery stairs descend down into the cave, giving you close-ups of fantastically shaped stalagmites and stalactites. They reminded ancient visitors of Greek gods and prompted them to erect stone altars and leave bronze votive offerings. Some are now at Iraklion's Archaeological Museum.

Cretan Wines. Long neglected among wine connoisseurs, Cretan wine is finally coming into its own, thanks to a new generation of wine makers. Your Cretan meals will be made unforgettable by copious amounts of delicious nectar, and you'll find wineries all over Crete (look for the burgundy-red road signs), with the greatest concentration in the **Iraklion Wine Country**. Nearly 80% of all wine produced on Crete comes from these rolling hills south of Knossos, especially from the towns of **Peza** and **Archanes**. Many wineries are now open to visitors for cellar tours and tastings. Try wines made from such indigenous varietals as the red Liatiko, the white Vilana or the once nearly extinct Dafni.

Other wine-producing regions include the northeastern part of the Lassithi region, namely around Sitia—where the **Toplou Monastery** especially has been producing high-quality wine for centuries—and the prefecture of Chania, famous for the Cretan Wine Festival held each summer in the village of **Ano Vouves**. For further information on Cretan wines, see www.newwinesofgreece.com and www.winesofcrete.gr.

Fresco in the Byzantine church of Panagia Kera in the village of Kritsa.

The East

The Dikti Mountains separate central Crete from the island's slender and thinly populated eastern section. An attractive port, plenty of entertainment, fine shopping and good restaurants make Agios Nikolaos the undisputed centre of vacation activity. Nearby Elounda has reportedly the highest density of five-star hotels, making it a favourite with celebrities. Offshore, the former leper colony on the island of Spinalonga is a major sightseeing stop in these parts.

A change of pace

Life moves slower along the Cretan Riviera, which extends east of Agios Nikolaos all the way to the dreamy palm beach at Vaï. The main town here is Sitia, which has remained a low-key holiday destination despite its fine sandy beach. The same is true of Ierapetra, the only sizeable town on the south coast, which has ferries to the unpopulated Chrissi Island. Archaeology fans should steer towards the Minoan palace at Kato Zakros or the intriguing hillside village of Gournia.

Agios Nikolaos

On a hilly peninsula jutting out into the graceful curve of the Gulf of Mirabello, Agios Nikolaos is a modern resort town with plenty of character and an ideal base for exploring the eastern part of Crete.

The Harbour

A focal point of activity, the harbour is also the starting point for cruises around Mirabello Bay. At night, a string of chic café-bars teems with young locals and visitors. The partly pedestrianised streets near the waterfront are handy for picking up crafts and souvenirs. A highlight is Byzantio, the icon workshop of Nikolaos Tziris.

The harbour is linked by a channel to the enigmatic **Lake Voulismeni**, which is lined with tourist-geared bars and tavernas. Many legends are associated with this circular landmark, which was thought to be bottomless until the British measured its depth (64 m) in 1953. A staircase in the back of the lake leads up to a viewpoint for a heavenly harbour panorama.

Archaeological Museum

Agios Nikolaos' well-respected archaeological collection on Paleologou Street has been closed for renovation for several years, but may reopen in 2015. It houses a small but choice collection of finds from throughout eastern Crete, going back to Neolithic times and ending with the Greco-Roman period. These include Minoan gold and ivory jewellery, bronze weapons, carved shells, terracotta figurines and stone and ceramic pottery.

As the sun goes down, take a *volta* along the quayside promenades.

Folk Museum
Right by the harbour and next to the tourist office, this little exhibit presents some fine woven carpets, musical instruments, ceramics and other traditional items.

Around Agios Nikolaos
This coastal town is an excellent base for excursions both along the coast and into the mountains.

Elounda
Chic coastal resorts line up like pearls along the road to Elounda, about 10 km (6 miles) north of Agios Nikolaos. Nevertheless, the small town itself has retained the down-to-earth character of a fishing village. There's a small sandy beach as well as plenty of excellent tavernas along the waterfront.

Spinalonga Island (Kalidon)
Elounda is the main staging ground for boat excursions to Spinalonga or Kalydon Island (near the Spinalonga Peninsula). Its 16th-century Venetian fortress harboured a leper colony from 1903 to 1957. As many as 1,000 Greeks were once kept here in isolation. The exhibits and largely ruined buildings, including the disinfection room and the hospital, are now protected as a national memorial. Walk around here is an eye-opening journey into this sad chapter of Greek history. Ferries to Spinalonga also leave from Agios Nikolaos and from Plaka to the north.

Kritsa
This mountain village, 12 km (7.5 miles) inland from Agios Nikolaos, is renowned for its weasing cottage industry. Bed- and table-linen, rugs and shawls are sold in the doorways of the workshops where they are made.

On the outskirts of Kritsa, in a charming setting amid cypress trees, is the whitewashed church of Panagia Kera (Sacred Virgin). It is revered for its exquisite Byzantine frescoes of the 14th and 15th centuries. On the ceiling of the dome are scenes from the life of Jesus. The Last Supper is depicted over the nave.

Istro Beaches
The coastal stretch just south of Agios Nikolaos is among the most dramatically scenic in all of Crete. This is where the Thripti

Mountains tumble all the way down to the cobalt blue Mediterranean. A trio of gorgeous beaches awaits near the village of **Istro**. Of these, crescent-shaped **Voulisma Beach** is the most stunning, with shallow, crystal-clear water, fine golden sand, beach chair rentals, a cafeteria and jet-ski and boat rentals. Unfortunately, it can get very busy in summer.

Gournia
The ancient Minoan village of Gournia drapes over a hill by the side of the highway, just 18 km (11 miles) southeast of Agios Nikolaos. Ancient cobbled walkways wind up the hillside past the ruins of tightly packed houses. Most had two stories, with stores, storage areas and workshops on the bottom and the living quarters at the top. Keep an eye out for remains of the external staircases that led to the second floor. They may well have been precursors to the traditional houses in Crete's mountain villages today, with rooftop sleeping arrangements.

Following the path to the top of the hill gets you to an open courtyard, which was the centre of public life. On the north side, a set of wide stairs points to the entrance of a palace, probably administrative centre and residence of the town leader. An upright slab west of the courtyard has been interpreted as a "sacred stone".

Sitia
This laid-back port town towards the eastern end of the island becomes crowded only at the height of the holiday season. Otherwise it's a charming, low-key alternative to the jammed north coast resorts with a wide promenade giving way to a long sandy beach.

Established as a prosperous trading port by the Venetians, Sitia was a frequent target for the voracious Algeria-based pirate Barbarossa, as well as earthquakes. A devastating Turkish blockade left the town in ruins in the 17th century and it recovered only 200 years later.

The Waterfront
The harbour offers an attractive collection of colourfully painted houses, shops, cafés and restaurants and gets particularly lively when locals come out for their evening stroll *(volta)*.

Out in the water, just beyond the buildings of the Port Authority, excavations have revealed ancient Roman fish tanks carved out of the rock.

Archaeological Museum
Sitia's collection includes finds from the region's prehistoric, Minoan and Greco-Roman archaeological sites, notably fine ceramics, a wine press from the Minoan palace of Kato Zakros, and intriguing ancient fishing

Just a short stroll from the crowded beach of Vaï you'll have only the goats for company.

equipment. Pride of place goes to a human figure (known as the **Palekastro Kouros**) made from hippopotamus ivory, wood, rock crystal and gold leaf.

Venetian Fort
With its splendid view over Sitia Bay and surrounding hills, the 16th-century fort—of which only the walls and a tower remain—provides the stage for occasional summer festivals of theatre and music. Another big event is the Sultana Raisin Festival in August, celebrating the annual harvest.

Moni Toplou
This popular excursion some 17 km (10 miles) east of Sitia takes you to an isolated fortress-like monastery. Its name translates as "canon" in reference to Venetian military efforts to defend the monastery in the 17th century. The church's prized treasure is one of the most precious icons in Crete: **Megas ei Kyrie** (Lord, Thou Art Great). Painted in late Byzantine style by Ioannis Kornaros (1745–96), it depicts 61 scenes from the Old and New Testaments. The monastery produces some of the finest olive oil on the island (available in the shop) and also operates its own winery.

Vaï
The palm-backed, sandy beach with rocky outcrops on the far north-eastern tip is one of Crete's most famous and is often deluged with day-trippers. According to legend, the trees grew from date pits left by Arab sailors in the 9th century, but in fact this particular palm species is endemic to Crete and does not produce edible fruit.

Kato Zakros
The road from Sitia offers a lovely drive across the eastern mountains' broad plateau to the village of **Zakros**. This is the jumping-off point for the hike through the dramatic **Zakros Gorge**, which ends at the palace ruins in the Bay of Kato Zakros.

Remains of the Minoan palace of Kato Zakros lie in a dramatic setting next to the beach in the far east corner of the island. Its sheltered harbour commanded the trade routes to Egypt and the Orient. As attested to by the splendid treasure of ivory and bronze now exhibited at Sitia's Archaeological Museum, the port commerce brought considerable prosperity. But the town's strategic location also gave it a vital military role in the island's defence, probably making Kato Zakros the Minoan kingdom's major naval base.

If you've explored Knossos or another Minoan palace, you may recognize the classical layout of such structures: a central courtyard flanked by a sanctuary and lustral basin on the west and royal apartments along the east side. Of special interest to the north of the courtyard are the remains of the royal kitchens, which were excavated with many utensils still practically intact.

The Minoan palace's plan is now believed to parallel, if not imitate, the Egyptian practice of building the apartments of the living on the side of the rising sun and the chapels devoted to immortality where the sun sets. Another Egyptian ritual may be mirrored in the Hall of the Cistern from which a stairway descends to a subterranean pool 7 m in diameter. Scholars suggest a sacred barque was floated here to enact the king's journey to the gods. But as other scholars suggest, it may just have been the royal swimming pool.

Ierapetra

The only town of any size on the south coast has a down-to-earth character, reasonably priced accommodation and a decent beach right in town. Its economy is rooted in fruit and vegetables grown for export in plastic-covered greenhouses that stretch pretty much along the entire coast here.

In town, the waterfront is lined with tavernas and bars and culminates at the well-restored 17th-century **Venetian fort** (called "Kales"), built by Francesco Morosini in 1626.

Nearby, the small **Archaeological Museum** in a former Turkish school presents the usual array of ancient ceramics, figurines, vases, tablets and other artefacts from Minoan times onwards. A beautifully painted Minoan sarcophagus deserves special attention, as does a 1.5 m high Roman statue of Persephone. Behind the museum, the charming lanes of the old Turkish quarter are worth a leisurely stroll.

Chrissi Island

Also known as Gaidouronisi Island, this uninhabited speck of land in the Mediterranean is a popular day trip from Ierapetra. In the summer, several boats daily embark on the 15-km (9-mile) journey to the island, which is famous for its large forest of Lebanon cedars. There's little to do here other than swimming, relaxing and snorkelling.

Once through the Iron Gates of Samaria Gorge you'll see the sea.

The West

Crete's West is the most untamed region on the island. It is anchored by two delightful towns, Rethimnon and Chania. The West is popular with individualists, and hikers are drawn by the trails of the White Mountains. Along the coast, fine beaches get a thumbs up from water sports aficionados. Mythology fans, meanwhile, will want to go on pilgrimage to the cave on Mt Psiloritis where Zeus was reared.

Rethimnon

An atmosphere of old-fashioned elegance continues to pervade the streets of a town that is still a favourite among Crete's students, writers and artists. It is on Rethimnon (also spelled Rethymno) rather than in Iraklion that they meet for discussions in the cafés below the Fortezza and other parts of the historic quarter.

This ambience has its origins in Rethimnon's golden era under the Venetians in the 15th and 16th centuries and remained largely intact even under the Turks. Besides converting a few churches into mosques by adding domes and minarets, the latter seem to have left behind mostly their delicious coffee. The Venetian heritage is still recaptured today by an annual summer festival of Renaissance music and theatre.

The Old Town

Rethimnon's labyrinthine historic quarter beautifully reflects both Venetian and Ottoman influences. The overhanging wooden balconies are typical Turkish additions to the arched stone façades of the Venetians. Wander into peaceful courtyards and you will see stately stone staircases climbing to upper apartments.

On Petichaki Street, the graceful square **Loggia** was once a gentlemen's club for the Venetian aristocracy. At the end of the street, on Petichaki Square, the **Rimondi Fountain** (1629) continues the Venetian-Turkish marriage of styles. Note the lions of St Mark between the Corinthian columns and vestiges of the Turkish dome.

On the square's south end, a slender minaret and three domes grace the **Neratze Mosque**, converted from the Venetian Church of Santa Maria and now a music school and concert venue.

Heading south on Ethnikis Antistaseos Street takes you to the public gardens via the 16th-century **Porta Guora**, named after Rector J. Guora, the only remaining stone gate of the Venetian town wall.

The Waterfront

Hemming the historic centre, the **Venizelou Promenade** follows the gentle curve of the sandy municipal beach. It is lined with open-air bars and cafés that are as popular with tourists during the daytime as they are with youthful locals in the evening. North of the promenade, the **Venetian Harbour** is a photogenic jewel with an historic lighthouse looming above small fishing craft and sailboats.

Fortezza

On a promontory north of the Old Town looms Rethimnon's imposing 16th-century fortress. It was built by the Venetians as a bulwark against Turkish assaults, but nonetheless captured in 1646 after a mere 22-day siege. From the ramparts you can enjoy a superb view over the harbour and the old city. Besides the soldiers' barracks, artillery and ammunition stores, the grounds originally encompassed a cathedral, a hospital and storage rooms.

Of the few surviving remnants the most notable is the domed **Sultan Ibrahim Mosque**, which was converted from the Venetian cathedral. Rethimnon's summertime Renaissance festival is held in the **Erofili Theatre** within the Fortezza grounds.

The Museums

The old Turkish prison next to the Fortezza houses Rethimnon's **Archaeological Museum**. Its prehistoric collection includes Stone and Bronze Age jewellery, tools and funeral ornaments. From Minoan and ancient Greek times come sculpted deities and other cult objects, some found in the Ideon Cave where Zeus was reared.

In a lovely 17th-century mansion, the **Historical & Folklore Museum** on Vernardou Street presents a selection of traditional arts and crafts, including jewellery, woven textiles, basketware, farm tools and household utensils.

In keeping with Rethimnon's artistic tradition, there's also the **Museum of Contemporary Art of Crete** on Chimaras below the Fortezza, which opens a window onto the contemporary arts scene in Crete and beyond.

Excursions from Rethimnon

Depending on how early you start out from Rethimnon, these destinations can be tackled separately or combined in one long day trip.

Moni Arkadiou

About 25 km (15 miles) southeast of Rethimnon, Arkadi Monastery is the supreme symbol of Crete's armed resistance against the Turks in the 19th century. Past the gated entrance, eyes are drawn to the elegant Venetian-style church with its ornate Renaissance façade and triple bell tower. To the left is the Refectory, still riddled with bullet holes and now a small museum. The gunpowder used in destroying the compound was stored in the now roofless

"Freedom or death". The brutally defiant slogan of Crete's fight against its oppressors is epitomized by the tragedy of **Arkadi Monastery**. It was here on November 9, 1866, that Abbot Gabriel holed up with guerrilla fighters defending hundreds of women and children. Outnumbered by the Turkish army, they awaited the final assault before the abbot gave the order to blow up the stores of gunpowder. The explosion killed several hundred Turkish soldiers along with the abbot and Cretan villagers themselves. Religious services still celebrate the anniversary in Rethimnon and Arkadi. The event is watered by tears and wine, the gunpowder recalled by fireworks, and it all ends in exuberant folk-dancing.

room in the far left corner. Outside, a former windmill has been turned into an **ossuary** with skulls of some of the victims neatly displayed behind glass.

Amari Valley

This excursion around the foothills of Mount Ida, southeast of Rethimnon, will please nature- and art-lovers alike. Tucked amid meadows and olive groves are many fine churches dating back beyond the Venetian era to Byzantine and even Early Christian times. Among them is the Panagia church of **Platania**, which has some good 15th-century frescoes. Even more impressive are those at the 14th-century Panagia Chapel in **Thronos** as they combine the austere Byzantine style with a more down-to-earth Venetian realism. Outside on the terrace are mosaics from the basilica that occupied the site in the 4th century. On the southern outskirts of Thronos, a 15-minute walk through the fields brings you to the ancient Greek acropolis of **Sybrita** (modern Syvritos).

Other notable frescoes are at the church of Archistrategos in **Monastiraki**. Some of Crete's oldest frescoes (1225) are in **Amari** itself at the church of Agia Anna in a lovely setting buried in the woods.

Near **Vizari** you'll spot the picturesque ruin of an Early Christian basilica (6th century). Con-

Crete has more than 200 species of orchid, including *Orphrys Cretica*.

Archaeologists excavated jewellery, bronze shields, drums and other votive offerings, now exhibited in the archaeological museums of Iraklion and Rethimnon.

The entrance to the cave, which is really just a big dark hole, is about 1 km from the car park at the top of the **Nida Plateau**. Sitting at an elevation of 1,400 m, it is reached via a paved road that corkscrews up the mountain for 22 km (13 miles). The views along the way are most beautiful in May or June when poppies, exotic orchids, dragon lilies and other wildflowers blanket the hillsides. A gruelling path, which is part of the **E4 Hiking Trail**, continues to the summit of Mt Psiloritis in about three hours.

tinuing a little higher gets you to **Fourfouras** for a grand view of the Libyan Sea beyond the Messara Plain. Fourfouras is also a jumping off point for climbs up Mt Ida.

Psiloritis (Mount Ida)

Mount Ida, officially known as Psiloritis ("the tall one"), is Crete's highest peak—2,456 m. According to mythology, Rea raised Zeus in its **Ideon Cave** (Idaion Antron) to hide him from his offspring-devouring father Cronus. The Greeks turned the cave into a pilgrimage sanctuary.

Anogia

Anogia is a good staging ground for exploring Mt Psiloritis and a worthy destination in its own right. The traditional village is famous as a centre of resistance and was twice destroyed by the Ottomans, in 1822 and 1867. The Nazis too, burned down the village in 1944, as reprisal for helping Allies in the kidnapping of a German general. Anogia is also the centre of stockbreeding in Crete and some of the elderly women still produce woven blankets and embroidered textiles. The village is also the birthplace of Nikos Xylouris (1936–80), Crete's most famous lyra player. His tiny home is now a museum.

Moni Preveli
In a stunning setting high above the Libyan Sea, this working monastery sheltered Cretan resistance fighters during the Ottoman occupation and also played a crucial role in the evacuation of Allied soldiers during World War II. A monument along the road leading up to the compound pays tribute to these acts of courage. So does a small exhibit in the onsite museum, which also houses exquisite icons dating from the 16th to the 19th centuries. Treasures inside the church include a fine gilded iconostasis and an ornate pulpit.

Preveli Beach
Below Moni Preveli, a steep path zigzags down to this celebrated sandy sliver at the mouth of the muscular Kourtaliotiko Gorge. The beach is justly famous for its grove of rare palm trees that extends about 1 km up the bed of the Megalopotamos river.

Plakias
Some 10 km (6 miles) west of Preveli, the Plakias resort spreads along a beach of grey sand and pebbles. Further east you can bathe at the sheltered **Damnoni Beach**.

Chania
Many visitors consider Chania (also spelled Hania, Khania or Canea) Crete's most attractive town thanks to its charming historical core that unites the best of its Venetian and Turkish eras. The town was the capital of Crete from 1898 to 1971 and stands on the site of Kydonia, an ancient Minoan city recorded in the stone tablets of Knossos as being founded by Kydon, the grandson of King Minos.

Venetian Harbour
In the graceful sweep of its natural harbour, Chania can claim the most attractive waterfront on the island. To embrace the scintillating panorama, take an early morning stroll along the breakwater out to the lighthouse. Come back at sunset and you will see that the colours have changed from ivory to amber and gold, deepening as the twinkling lights of the tavernas and boutiques come on for the evening trade.

The port divides into two, with the Inner Harbour to the east and the Outer Harbour to the west. At the west end of the Outer Harbour, Firkas Fortress, part of the Venetian fortifications, has been restored to house the **Maritime Museum of Crete**, which traces Greek maritime history. Among the exhibits are models of ancient

Painterly charm in a back street of Chania.

Greek triremes and an account of the World War II-era Battle of Crete.

Across the water looms the elegant dome of Chania's oldest surviving Turkish building, the former **Janissaries' Mosque** (Yiali Jami) of 1645, which houses the occasional art exhibit.

East of the mosque, the old **Venetian Arsenals** are the most striking feature of the Inner Harbour; barrel-vaulted warehouses that constituted the shipyards for refitting and arming the Venetian fleet.

Archaeological Museum

This stellar collection of artefacts from Neolithic to Roman times is beautifully presented within the high-ceiling Venetian church of a former Franciscan monastery. Highlights include Minoan sculpture, sarcophagi and clay tables with Linear A and Linear B script, a marble bust of Emperor Hadrian, Roman mosaic floors and Greek vases. In the garden you can still see the Turkish wellhouse and a fragment of a minaret from the monastery's days as a mosque.

Kastelli Quarter

The hill behind the Janissaries' Mosque is the oldest part of Chania. Around the former church of Agia Ekaterini, which was destroyed by German bombs in World War II, archaeologists have found traces of the Minoan settlement of **Kydonia**. These include the foundations of several villas as well as, perhaps, the royal palace itself. The most important finds, including exquisite vases, are now displayed in Chania's Archaeological Museum.

Topanas Quarter

In the narrow streets behind the Firkas Fortress, the main Turkish neighbourhood is easily recognised by the wooden balconies and mansard roofs attached to

Venetian stone houses. Its narrow lanes teem with charming cafés, B&Bs and boutiques, especially along **Theotokopoulou Street**. At its north end, the **Church of Agios Salvatore** (or San Salvatore) contains a fine collection of Byzantine and post-Byzantine artefacts, art and jewellery as well as an impressive mosaic floor.

Evraiki Quarter
South of Topanas, behind the Archaeological Museum, is Chania's former Jewish (Evraïká) quarter. The **Etz Hayyim Synagogue** is the only tangible reminder of what was once a flourishing local Jewish community. It's at the end of a narrow walkway off Kondilaki Street and is open to the public.

Splantzia Quarter
East of the Archaeological Museum, Splantzia's main sightseeing attraction is the **Church of Agios Nikolaos**, which sports both a bell-tower and a minaret.

Shoppers will be drawn to **Skridlof Lane** for its extensive selection of leather products, and to the covered **Agora**, the traditional market hall, which nowadays caters more to souvenir-hunting tourists.

Historical Archive and Museum
On Sfakianaki St, this exhibit presents Venetian maps, documents and furniture but is primarily a patriotic homage to Cretan struggles for independence. A formidable array of weapons accompanies portraits of the island's heroic fighters against Turks and Germans. Pride of place is accorded to prime minister Eleftherios Venizelos, who was born near Chania in 1864.

Akrotiri Peninsula
Punching out northeast of Chania like a giant fist, the Akrotiri peninsula cradles the superb natural harbour of Souda Bay. If you come in to Chania by ferry, this is the port of call. The sailors' bars and cafés are boisterous in the evenings as Souda serves as a base for NATO and the Greek navy. Overlooking the bay is also a British War Cemetery for the soldiers who died in the Crete campaign of 1941. On the peninsula itself, north of the Chania International Airport, NATO operates a missile firing range (NAMFI).

Although the idyll is marred by the military presence, Akrotiri is not without natural charms and cultural appeal.

Profitis Ilias Hill
Up on Profitis Ilias Hill, in a suitably grand location, are the simple tombs of Greek Prime Minister Eleftherios Venizelos and his son Sofoclis. They are

both buried on a historic site of Cretan rebellion against the Turks in 1897. The hill also offers a splendid view over Chania and its bay.

Stavros

Film buffs will recognise the nicest beach on the peninsula as the place where the famous dance scene in the movie Zorba the Greek, starring Anthony Quinn, was shot. Put down your towel in this nearly circular bay, hemmed in by a peninsula with coves, a fine sandy beach and emerald-green water.

Monasteries

Akrotiri is home to three monasteries. The Renaissance-style **Moni Agia Triada** (Monastery of the Holy Trinity) was built in the 17th century by two Venetian brothers who converted to the Orthodox Church. Its church has richly ornamented choir stalls and restored icons. The monks sell wine and olive oil.

A paved road climbs 4 km (2.5 miles) to the fortress-like 16th-century **Moni Gouverneto**, famous for its façade which is lavishly decorated with columns, ornaments and monstrous figures. Inside the monastery, a precious icon tells the story of a 10th-century hermit named John, who lived in the gorge below the monastery.

A steep trail leads down to his cave as well as to the ruins of **Moni Katholiko** in about 45 minutes.

Along the Coast

Driving away from Chania you will pass by fabulous beach resorts which also serve as good bases for exploring the fishing villages and monasteries on the craggy west and southwest coastlines. On the south coast also lie two famous gorges, Samaria and Imbros.

Maleme

In the more sombre days of World War II, this now very well-equipped beach resort was a major focus of the German invasion—Chania's nearby airfield was the island's principal air base for the allies at the time. At their cemetery of more than 4,000 graves, just inland from the coastal highway, the Germans have erected a monument to their heroism, still visited by nostalgics of the ferocious ten-day Battle of Crete fought in 1941. The cheerful resort hotels, tennis courts and swimming pools make a stark and welcome contrast.

Kastelli Kissamou

Also known simply as Kissamos, this town's antecedents are the Greco-Roman city state of Kissamos and a Venetian trading post. Numerous archaeological vestiges have been excavated and are now displayed in the **Archaeological Museum** housed in a former governor's palace. Today, Kissamos' main draws are its long stretches of sandy beach and the casual atmosphere of its tavernas. It is also a good base for boat excursions to the Venetian island fortress of Gramvousa and the lovely Balos Lagoon as well as day trips to Elafonissi beach.

Idyllic view over the Balos Lagoon on the Gramvousa Peninsula.

Gramvousa Peninsula

West of Kissamos rises the uninhabited Gramvousa Peninsula, which is home to two fabulous beaches. Near its northwestern tip lies the remote **Balos Lagoon**, whose shallow waters shimmer in shades from sky blue to turquoise and are fringed by dunes and sparkling powdery sand.

Excursion boats from Kissamos drop off large numbers of sun worshippers in summer. Boats first stop at the island of **Imeri Gramvousa**, where a steep path leads up to the ruins of a Venetian fortress. To enjoy Balos without the crowds, you need to drive here in the early morning or late afternoon via a 13-km (8-mile) long graded dirt road, which starts near Kaliviani.

Not quite as exotic but easier to reach are the secluded coves and the long dune-backed **Falassarna Beach** at the southern end of the Gramvousa Peninsula. Aside from a handful of tavernas, bars and little shops, there is hardly any infrastructure here. After the paved road ends, a graded dirt road continues for 2 km (1.5 miles) to the excavated vestiges of what was once a prosperous trade port in the 4th century BC.

Moni Chrisoskalitissa

This 17th-century monastery is spectacularly located atop a rock overlooking the southwest corner of the island. Inside are a small museum with faded icons and old manuscripts as well as a recreated monk's cell. One of its 90 steps is supposedly made of pure gold — but only the pure-hearted can see it.

Elafonissi

Tucked into the island's southwestern corner, Elafonissi ranks among Crete's most spectacular beaches. Its crystal-clear, shallow waters and pink-shimmering sand bring to mind the Caribbean.

The setting is made all the more stunning by the **Elafonissi Islet**, which lies just 50 m offshore. In summer, the beach is usually deluged with day trippers, so come early or late in the day to avoid the worst crowds. The entire area is protected as part of the European Union's Natura 2000 project.

Paleochora

This relaxed south-coast town occupies an enviable peninsula location and is flanked by both a long sandy and a pebbly beach. It has a ruined Venetian castle, bouncing nightlife in its harbourside tavernas and some pleasant small hotels for an overnight stay.

In summer, there's a daily ferry to the pink-hued beach of Elafonissi. You can also sail to the old pirate's haunt of **Gavdos**, geographically the southernmost point of Europe. The island is the mythological home of the sea nymph Calypso, who held Odysseus hostage for seven years while his wife Penelope patiently wove and unravelled her tapestry, waiting for his return.

Sougia

Little more than a cluster of white houses hugging a long beach of grey sand and small pebbles, low-key Sougia has retained Cretan authenticity and appeals to those seeking peace and quiet amid lovely scenery. The waterfront promenade has some excellent fish tavernas.

Samaria Gorge

The hike down this grandiose gorge through the Lefka Ori (White Mountains) ranks as one of Crete's most exhilarating outdoor experiences. The rollicking trek extends 16 km (10 miles) down to the most welcome of refreshing dips in the Libyan Sea at the village of Agia Roumeli. Wear a good pair of hiking shoes and bring sunblock and a hat. In summer, heavy crowds can detract from the experience. The trailhead is in Omalos, easily reached by car or the early morning bus from Chania. A small entrance fee is charged. For the return journey, you need to take a short boat trip from Agia Roumeli to Chora Sfakion from where a bus will carry you back to Chania.

If you do not feel up to the whole hike, you can still do it the "Lazy Way" by starting at Agia Roumeli and exploring the southern end of the Samaria Gorge. To get there, catch the morning bus from Chania to Chora Sfakion and from there the ferry to Agia Roumeli. The Iron Gates, the narrowest section of the gorge, are about a one-hour hike away.

TREKKING IN CRETE

Numerous canyons slice through Crete's mountainous interior that are crowd-free but just as beautiful as the rugged Samaria Gorge, the longest and most famous. Most of them can be explored without a guide, but bring plenty of water, sustenance and sunscreen. Always take time to check road and weather conditions locally before setting out.

Imbros Gorge. Samaria's "little sister" winds 7 km (4 miles) past soaring cliffs, natural arches, caves and fragrant herbs. Its narrowest point is just 1.6 m wide. The trailhead is in the village of Imbros, a stop on Chania bus route. The gorge spills out at Komitades; from there it is another 5 km (3 miles) on foot or by taxi down to the sea to Chora Sfakion, where you can take the return bus to Chania or Rethymnon.

Zakros Gorge. The last 8 km (5 miles) of the 10,000 km (6,213 miles) long E4 European Long Distance Path run from the town of Zakros through the spectacular gorge also known as "Valley of the Dead" thanks to its Minoan cave tombs. The relatively easy, well-signposted trail ends at the beach, near the Minoan palace of Kato Zakros.

Rouvas Gorge. This moderately strenuous 5 km (3 mile) hike kicks off at Lake Votomos in Zaros at the southern foothills of Mt Ida. The trailhead passes Moni Agios Nikolaos (Saint Nicholas Monastery), which hides a chapel with 14th-century frescoes among hulking modern buildings. Increasingly steep, the path culminates at the little chapel of Agios Ioannis (St. John).

Omalos

The White Mountain village Omalos is the "launch pad" for Samaria hikers. There are cafés and small shops to stock up on food and water. There is no food along the trail, but there are water taps where you can refill your bottle. Toilets and rest stops are available as well.

The Trail

The trail starts with a steep descent into the gorge via a stony path outfitted with a wooden handrail *(Xyloskalon)*. With the towering chasm of Mount Gingilos looming to the right, it slopes steeply down some 1,000 m to what is not the bottom but only the upper ledge of the gorge. The path gets a little easier once you reach the **Chapel of Agios Nikolaos**, sitting pretty amid tall pines and cypresses. The mountainsides sparkle in shades of silver, emerald and blue, while the cool waters of the pools provide a refreshing break.

About half way, you'll come upon the abandoned hamlet of Samaria and the 14th-century **Chapel of Ossia Maria** (St Mary's Chapel), which gives Samaria its name.

Further on, the trail tapers dramatically until it reaches its narrowest point (3.5 m) at **Sideroportes** (Iron Gates) near the 11 km mark. Here, the gorge almost closes in on itself with rock walls soaring high above you. From the "gates", it is another 4 km (2.5 miles) to the open sea at Agia Roumeli.

Agia Roumeli

The beach here, lapped by the gentle waves of the Libyan Sea, is the just reward for hardy hikers as is a refuelling stop at a local taverna.

Before reaching the village of Agia Roumeli, you'll pass by the **Panagia Church**, which shares its site with a Greek temple to Apollo—note the ancient mosaic in the forecourt.

Sirtaki. We think of it as the quintessential Greek folk dance, but in fact the famous Sirtaki was only invented in 1964 during the filming of *Zorba the Greek*, starring Anthony Quinn. Since the actor was injured during filming, he was unable to perform quick movements, so choreographer Giorgos Provias had to improvise the famous dance scene shot at Stavros Beach. He found inspiration in authentic Greek dances, most notably the *hasapiko*. This line dance, in which dancers put their hands on their neighbours' shoulders, was originally performed by the medieval butchers guild in Constantinople.

Loutro

This picture-perfect coastal village is a crescent of sparkling white houses festooned with blue shutters and vibrant flowers. It lies halfway between Agia Roumeli and Chora Sfakion and is only accessible on foot or by boat. The beach in town is small and pebbly, but several much better ones are just a hike, canoe ride or boat taxi ride away. Another trail leads uphill to the mountain village of **Anopolis**.

Chora Sfakion

Chora Sfakion is at the heart of the Sfakia region, whose people are known all over Greece for their bravery — and legendary ferocity — in the guerrilla struggles against the Ottomans. Their great hero in the 1770 rebellions was Ioannis Vlachos, better known by his nickname Daskalogiannis. There's a monument to him in the town of Anopolis, in the hills above Chora Sfakion.

The village itself is mostly notable for its taverna-lined waterfront and as the departure point for coastal hikes to secluded beaches such as **Glyka Nera** (meaning "Sweet Water" in Greek), which is also served daily by a small ferry.

Chora Sfakion is also the eastern terminus of the ferry service to the villages along the rugged south coast, including Loutro, Agia Roumeli (for the Samaria Gorge), Sougia and Paleochora. Ferries to Gavdos Island, the southernmost point in Europe, also depart from here.

Imbros Gorge

The hike here is easier than Samaria, the paths less steep, but the mountainous landscape is just as theatrical, and nature-lovers claim that the array of wild flowers in springtime is even more impressive. Imbros is also less popular than Samaria and so less crowded at high season.

Take the bus from Chania to the village of **Imbros**. The southward hike through the gorge's dried-up riverbed covers a distance of 7 km (4 miles) and, with short rest stops along the way, takes about three hours. There's a small fee.

Just short of the sea, the terminus for the gorge is the village of **Komitades**. Visit the church of St George here to see the 14th-centuries frescoes.

Frangokastello

Some 15 km (9 miles) east of Chora Sfakion, this grand 14th-century Venetian fort is the local focus of Sfakiot heroics. Its four towers bear silent witness to the insurgents massacred here by the Turkish army in 1828. The other reason to visit is the grand sweep of family-friendly sandy beach.

THE BACKDROP

Byzantine Art
Entirely religious in subject matter, Byzantine painting has always obeyed a strict formality noticeable in the frescoes adorning the walls of holy places and in the style of icons. In the churches, the main dome is always reserved for Christ Pantocrator, the Almighty, shown seated or standing and in a commanding position; on the lower walls follow, in hierarchical order, the angels, the prophets, the four Evangelists and the bishops.

Under the rounded vault of the apse, the Virgin Mary appears, often accompanied by the archangels Michael and Gabriel, sometimes enthroned, perhaps with the infant Jesus on her knees, or with her hands raised in prayer. The icons are displayed on the iconostasis in precise positions: the Virgin Mary on the left, Jesus on the right, Saint John and the saint to whom the church is dedicated on the sides. After the 12th century, artists began plating icons with worked metal (usually silver) with only the face and hands of the subject uncovered.

The stylised attitudes and classically formal faces respond to Byzantine rules of aesthetics, seeking to evoke the divine by avoiding any hint of a personality. Crete was long neglected by Constantinople and stayed true to this tradition until a new, more expressive style with a more pronounced use of colour, emerged during the Venetian occupation. One of its greatest practitioners was the 16th-century Cretan icon painter Michail Damaskinos, who was visibly influenced by his five-year stay in Venice.

The Olive
The emblem of Greece and symbol of the Mediterranean basin, the olive tree was offered by the goddess Athena to the people placed under her protection. Sophocles and his contemporaries held the tree in high regard, comparing the colour of its leaves to that of Athena's eyes.

The sacred nature of the olive derives from its many uses. Aside from being tasty and nutritious, its oil also served as fuel for lamps and for massaging the bodies of athletes. Probably originating in Africa, the tree seems to have grown on Crete long before the first settlers arrived. Thanks to the key role it played in commercial exchange, it also contributed to the emergence of the Greek civilisation.

The tree can live for seven centuries, but it needs to grow for many years before the first fruit can be harvested. A saying goes that if the father plants the tree, the son harvests the fruit and the grandson makes the oil. The harvest takes place in winter, starting traditionally on St Dimitri's Day, October 26, and ending in late February.

Orthodox Church
After a series of disputes in the 9th to 11th centuries, the official church of the Holy Roman Empire split in 1054 into Eastern (Greek) and Western (Latin) branches, which evolved into the Eastern Orthodox Church and the Roman Catholic Church. The beliefs remain similar, although there's a major point of divergence concerning the Holy Ghost. In the Orthodox (from the Greek orthos, belief, and doxa, true) interpretation, it proceeds only "from the Father", while the Catholic creed follows the Latin text, "from the Father and the Son".

The Orthodox church has several variants and no supreme authority the way the Catholics have a pope. It is divided into several national communities led by patriarchs. Nowadays about 97 per cent of the Greek population are Orthodox. Religion is an important part of the national identity and held the people together during the Ottoman occupation. It is taught in schools and mentioned on the national identity card.

Script
The Minoans were the first civilisation in the Europe to develop a form of writing. The first hieroglyphic script, undeciphered to this day, appeared at the beginning of the Bronze Age, the best-known example being imprinted on the clay Phaistos disk. The syllabic system that followed, known as Linear A, also remains a mystery. It was mostly used in palace and religious writings of the Minoans.

Linear B appeared after the invasion of Crete by the Myceneans from mainland Greece around 1400 BC. It is considered an early version of modern-day Greek. Some 4,000 tablets have been found, many of them in the palace archives of Knossos and Kydonia (today's Chania). Most record commercial transactions or inventories.

Take home your own Phaistos Disk and see if you can decipher it.

SHOPPING

The challenge on any Greek island these days is finding the good quality gift, preferably handmade, among the profusion of cheap and not-so-cheap mass-produced souvenirs. Unless, of course, you have a well-developed collector's taste for kitsch, in which case you will have plenty to choose from.

Where to buy
Iraklion has predictably the largest selection of products coming in from all over the island, but the maze-like old quarters of Chania and Rethimnon offer more character in their delightful galleries, artesanal shops, organic food stores and boutiques. There's an entire leather lane in Chania as well. A few mountain villages keep up such cottage-industry traditions as embroidery and textile weaving. The wine country near Iraklion is great for sampling and picking up a bottle or two.

Antiques & Icons
Officially, anything dating from before Greek Independence in 1821 is accorded the status of "antique". To export a genuine antique, you will need a permit—and you're not likely to get one.

Good copies of classic icons are sold in many galleries and shops close to major churches, as well as in museum shops and monasteries. There are several excellent icon painters on Crete these days, including Nikos Tziris who operates his workshop Byzantio in Agios Nikolaos.

Ceramics
Vases and fruit dishes echo the ancient Minoan styles with vivid scenes from the dancing and bull-leaping legends of Knossos, classical geometric patterns, and woven or lacy cut-out designs. At Atelier Ceramica in Agios Nikolaos, Nic Gabriel specialises in stunningly precise handmade copies of antique vases. The rural tradition continues unbroken in robust oil jars and wine jugs still handmade in the village of Thrapsano, about 30 km (18 miles) southeast of Iraklion. The village of Margarites is famous for its fine painted ceramics; it's 25 km (15 miles) east of Rethimnon.

Embroidery and Textiles

The embroidered shawls and table linen of Kritsa have gained fame well beyond the shores of Crete. Anogia too does a roaring trade in textiles. Note that not everything is truly made locally: caveat emptor! If you're in the market for a genuine hand-woven carpet, swing by Roka Carpets in Chania.

In all the major resorts you'll find nicely finished goods—bedspreads and curtains, wall-hangings, pillow-cases and delicate handkerchiefs and doilies. Heavy woollen sweaters may also be a good bargain. Look, too, for the multicoloured woven wool shoulder bags known in Crete as *vourgia*.

Gourmet Gifts

Edible gifts make great souvenirs for friends and also help you reminisce about your fine Cretan holiday when back home. Crete produces superb olive oil as well as beauty products derived from it, such as soap, shampoo and body lotions. Toplou Monastery in eastern Crete is a top olive oil purveyor and also makes excellent wine. Delicious wine can also be tasted and purchased straight from the wineries in the Iraklion Wine Country, which starts in the hills just south of Knossos.

Popular sweets include baklava pastries, loukoum, nougat, dried fruit, and raisins or nuts preserved in brandy or honey.

Also stock up on dried herbs and spices, ideally not the pre-packaged kind in cellophane bags, but fresh ones gathered straight from the mountains. Special to Crete is dittany, a relative of oregano, which is also used for medicinal purposes.

The ubiquitous mountain tea is not only delicious but also said to be good for fighting everything from colds to indigestion.

Jewellery

Pieces inspired by classic Minoan or Byzantine designs are widely available, both made out of gold or silver or as costume jewellery. A particularly popular motif is the Minoan Bee, a pendant found at the Minoan palace of Malia.

Leatherware

Quality leather products are available throughout Crete and there are bargains to be had, especially when it comes to sandals, belts and handbags. Skridlof Lane in Chania is chock-a-block with vendors, but there are also some fine stores in Rethimnon and Iraklion.

Music

Instruments associated with classic Cretan music are the lyra, the laouto (lute) and the bouzouki. Aerakis Music in Iraklion specialises in recorded Cretan traditional music by old and new masters, many released on its own label. If you want to buy your own handmade instrument, try En Hordais in Rethimnon.

Souvenirs

Lurking behind the shop sign "Greek Art", you'll find a multitude of delightfully kitschy items ranging from bottles of ouzo disguised as Corinthian columns to multiple versions of the Phaistos Disk masquerading as pendants, key rings or cocktail mats.

Sponges are sold in the ports but might be imported from North Africa or Asia. The natural brown ones are longer-lasting than the yellow ones which have been bleached.

Wood

Olive wood has been carved since ancient times. Its knotty wood, in various shades, makes splendid salad bowls and trays, mortars and other kitchen utensils, jewellery boxes as well as *komboloï*, the traditional worry beads that you see Cretan men playing with all day long.

Catherine Gerber

Catherine Gerber

fotolia.com/Leimane

istockphoto.com/Stern

An olive oil tasting. | *Raki* or *tsikoudia*, a unique grape spirit | You can never have too many mugs! | Fascinate the children by teaching them that a sponge is an animal.

A few drops of olive oil are enough to make your Cretan salad a feast for the palate.

DINING OUT

With its emphasis on fresh fruit, vegetables, fish and herbs as well as farm-raised meats, grains and olive oil, the Cretan diet is considered among the healthiest in the world. Long before it became a worldwide food trend, Cretans sourced their food locally and preferred organic produce. Here you'll find outstanding restaurants and tavernas where you can enjoy authentic, delicious meals. Note that most locals don't eat lunch until about 2pm and dinner before 9pm or 10pm.

To Start With...

It's easy to make a complete meal out of a variety of starters called *meze* (plural *mezedes*). The parade usually begins with olives, black and green, plain or dressed in lemon, garlic, coriander or peppers. Then come the dips such as the ubiquitous *tzatziki* (yoghurt and cucumber, with mint or garlic), *hummus* (chickpea purée), *taramosalata* (smoked cod roe purée) or *melitzanosalata* (smoky eggplant or aubergine). Stuffed vine leaves are called dolmades and pickled cauliflower is moungra. Scoop these up with a piece of *paximadia* (rusk), *elioti* (olive bread) or *pita*, the slightly leavened flat bread.

The most prevalent salad is the highly-appreciated *choriatiki salata* (Greek salad), a bountiful bowl of tomatoes, cucumber, black olives, onions and thick wedges of feta cheese, all drizzled with fruity olive oil. If available, also try a salad made from freshly gathered mountains green (*horta*), although these are more commonly served boiled.

Top of the seafood list are *kalamari* (squid), served grilled or breaded and deep-fried, and *oktapodhi ksidhato* (thinly sliced and pickled octopus). Hot appetizers include *loukaniko* (pork, lamb or veal sausages), *saganaki* (fried cheese) and *tiropita* or *spanakopita*—flaky pastries stuffed with cheese or spinach, respectively.

Popular soups are *avgolemono* (egg and lemon), *psarosoupa* (fish soup) and *fasolada* (bean soup).

Main Course: Fish or Meat?

If you can still manage it, the most common fish dishes, baked, grilled or sautéed, are red mullet, sea bass, swordfish, sole, bream and sardines. Spiny lobster, shrimp and squid are likely to be frozen but can still be delicious when prepared grilled or in a local white wine and tomato sauce.

Stew (*stifado*), usually made with veal or beef but also with rabbit, is a robust dish. Pork, veal or lamb are also served spit-roasted and slivered (*gyros*, also known as doner kebab) or cut in cubes (*souvlakia*). Grilled steaks are brizoles. Lamb (sometimes mutton) is also served as simple chops (*païdakia*), oven-baked (*kleftiko*) or barbecued (*ofto*). In mountain villages, you will come across superb dishes made from *katsika* (goat). A delicacy for adventurous eaters is a plate of *saligaria* (snails); on the island, these are usually called *kohli*, spiral.

Clearly a Venetian legacy is Cretans' love for pasta, both as cheese-filled ravioli or spaghetti in a variety of meat-, tomato- and cheese-based sauces. *Pastitsio* is a rather earthy dish of baked macaroni layered with minced beef. *Moussaka* is also popular—layers of minced beef, potato and eggplant topped with béchamel sauce.

Desserts

A splendid sweet Venetian legacy is the delicate creamy rice pudding called *rizogalo*. This is usually topped with cinnamon. The local custard pie (*galaktoboureko*) and ice creams are pretty good, too.

Among the fresh fruit, enjoy whatever happens to be in season: melons, figs, pomegranates, apricots, peaches, oranges, grapes, etc.

Cretans are great fans of stopping by the pastry shop (*zaharoplastio*) after dinner to indulge in heavenly *baklava*, a flaky pastry stuffed with honey and nuts; *kataïfi* or *kanafeh*, a pastry made from shredded dough; *loukoumades*, which are doughnuts soaked in sugar syrup; or *kalitsounia*, small sweet pies stuffed with fresh cheese.

Drinks

The usual range of international beers is widely available, but do also try the excellent local brews such as *Mythos*, *Alpha* and *Fix*. There's also one microbrewery on Crete, the German-owned *Brink's Beer*, which is based near Rethymno and makes superb full-flavoured beer that is both organic and unfiltered.

For the longest time Crete was known only for its poor-quality bulk wine, but over the last 10 years a new generation of winemakers has started to turn things around. This has resulted in a growing number of respectable vintages, often featuring indigenous grapes such as *Vidiano*, *Liatiko*, *Kotsifali* and *Dafni*. The resinous *Retsina*, so popular in other parts of Greece, only plays a minor role on Crete.

The same can be said about *ouzo* since Cretans much prefer their traditional spirit in the form of *raki* (also called *tsikoudia*), which is seemingly drunk at all hours and on all occasions. In tavernas, it is often offered as a complimentary digestive. Raki is distilled from crushed grape skins and similar to Italian grappa. A stronger red-tinged variation called *mournoraki* is distilled from mulberries.

If you just ask for a coffee *(kafes)*, you will probably be served an instant Nescafé. The refreshing iced version is very popular in summer. Lovers of fresh coffee should order a thick black *elliniko*, made in a small coffee pot with a long handle. Served over its grounds, you can choose it without sugar (*sketo*), medium sweet (*metrio*) or sweeter (*glyko*).

The Greek taste: *tzatziki*, grilled fish, meat cooked on skewers, and *kalitsounia* cheese cakes for an afternoon snack.

Don't miss the chance to do some kayaking on the Kourtaliotis River.

SPORTS

There's no lack of sporting possibilities to keep your body as fit and supple as a Greek god or goddess.

Water Sports
Beaches in the north tend to be white or golden sand, while those on the south coast are often grayish and pebbly. Especially scenic beaches are those at Vaï, Elafonissi, Preveli, Falassarna and Triopetra.

Most resorts offer a wide range of water sports, including waterskiing, jet-skiing, windsurfing, parasailing, canoeing, kayaking and yachting. Facilities are usually open for non-resort guests as well. Many also provide equipment and instruction for scuba-diving and snorkelling. The attraction of Crete's offshore diving is to see not just marine life but also the remains of ancient submerged cities and Roman port installations, especially in the Gulf of Mirabello (Agios Nikolaos).

Fishing
Hire a boat at any of the resort harbours to go out for the dentex, sea bass or swordfish and have your hotel prepare your catch for supper. A license is technically required and should be supplied through your hotel or the boat operator.

Hiking
Crete is paradise for hikers, thanks to its many gorges, plateaus, mountains and coastal routes. In all major resorts you'll find operators offering guided hiking excursions to Samaria and other gorges. As a result, these routes tend to be busy, but there are plenty of others—shorter and less busy but no less scenic—that you can tackle on your own with some logistical planning. Serious hikers and climbers might want to get in touch with a local chapter of the Greek Mountaineering Association for advice on routes and refuges. They also organise guided tours.

Tennis
The luxury hotels have good asphalt or clay courts, but bring your own racquet. Other hotels can help you with temporary membership of the tennis clubs at Iraklion and Chania.

THE HARD FACTS

To plan your trip, here are some of the practical details you should know about Crete.

Airports
Most international flights arrive in Iraklion or Chania. For now, only domestic flights land in Sitia.

Holiday packages usually include bus transfer to your hotel. Otherwise, there are plenty of taxis (with standard rates posted beside the stand) and public transport to take you to most of the major resort towns.

Climate
Crete gets very hot in July and August with temperatures averaging 29°C (85°F). June and September are moderate and there's usually nice weather in March, April, October and early November. Rain is possible between October and March, when there's also snow in the mountains.

Crete is famous for its winds. The most common one is the northern summertime *meltemi*.

Communications
The mobile phone network is GSM 900/1800. If you have an unlocked phone, it may be cheaper to buy a prepaid local SIM card. Most towns and resorts have internet cafés, and many bars, cafés and hotels provide WiFi access (often free) to their guests.

Courtesy
Contact with locals is easier than you might imagine. In the towns, many speak some English, but a couple of words of Greek from you—*parakalo* (please) or *efharisto* (thank you)—are much appreciated. In churches, knees and shoulders should be covered. Being stared at is not perceived as rude but as a flattering sign of interest, as is asking personal questions about you or your family.

Crime
Crete has a very low crime rate, especially outside the cities. Of course, this doesn't mean you should let your guard down. Simply take the same common-sense precautions you would at home.

Driving
For car rentals you need a valid national licence as well as an International Driving Permit if you're from outside the EU. The

minimum age for rental is usually 21, although drivers under 25 may have to pay a surcharge. Local rental firms tend to be competitive in price with the major international companies.

Speed limits are 50 kph in villages, 90 kph outside towns and on the New Road on the north coast. The alcohol limit is 0.5‰. Seatbelts must be worn in front and back.

For most of its length, the north coast highway is in first rate condition. Drive on the right, overtake on the left. Country roads can be narrow, winding and slow, especially in the mountains, where sudden encounters with flocks of sheep and goats are not uncommon.

Electricity
Electric current is 220-volt 50-cycle AC for Continental European two-pin earthed plugs. Most hotel bathrooms have outlets for 220/110-Volt razors.

Emergencies
Most problems can be handled at your hotel desk. Apart from the general European emergency number, 112, you can dial 100 for the police, 199 for the fire brigade, 166 for an ambulance, 1016 for medical service and 171 for the tourist police. There is a British Consulate in Iraklion (others in Athens).

Formalities
Citizens of the EU, Norway, Iceland and Switzerland need only their national identity card or passport to enter Crete. US, Canadian and Australian nationals are among those that require only a valid passport but no Schengen Visa. Check details with your local Greek embassy.

Passengers over the age of 17 arriving from non-EU countries may import the following goods duty-free: 200 cigarettes or 50 cigars or 250 g tobacco products and 1 litre of spirits over 22° proof or 2 litres of other alcoholic beverages of 22° or less, and 4 litres wine and 16 litres beer.

Residents of EU countries may import the following amounts of tax-paid goods: 800 cigarettes or 200 cigars or 1 kg tobacco products; 10 litres of spirits over 22° or 20 litres of spirits under 22° or 90 litres wine or 110 litres beer.

Health
Sensitive stomachs may need to adjust to the Greek diet, but if you don't like oily foods, stick to simple grilled fish or meat and salads for which you fix your own dressing. Tap water is generally safe, but bottled water tastes better and is easy to find.

Residents of 28 European nations only need a European Health Insurance Card (EHIC) to receive low-cost or free emergency medical care. Cards are issued by your state health insurance provider. Everyone else should take out travel insurance that covers emergency holiday illnesses.

Holidays and festivals

Jan 1	New Year
Jan 6	Epiphany
March 25	Greek Independence Day
August 15	Assumption
Oct 28	"Ohi" Day ("No" Day), commemorating Greek resistance to Italian invasion in 1940
Dec 25	Christmas Day
Dec 26	St Stephen's Day

Movable:
1st Day of Lent (Clean Monday); Good Friday; Easter Monday; Ascension; Whit Monday.

Languages
English, German and Russian are the most commonly spoken languages after Greek. Street signs are usually written in Greek and Roman letters.

Money
The Greek unit of currency is the Euro, divided into 100 cents. Coins: 1, 2, 5, 10, 20 and 50 cents, 1 and 2 euros; banknotes: 5, 10, 20, 50, 100, 200 and 500 euros.

Public Transport
Buses are the only form of public transport on Crete. The network is extensive and services generally regular and quite punctual. At least hourly service connects the main north coast communities (Kissamos, Chania, Rethimnon, Iraklion, Agios Nikolaos and Sitia), with less frequent buses to the villages in the mountains and on the south coast. Most major attractions, including the archaeological sites, are also served. If you are planning a hike in the country, check on bus schedules for the return journey (www.bus-service-crete-ktel.com).

Taxis, individual or shared, are efficient, honest and reasonable in price.

Tipping
A service charge is included, by law, in hotel and restaurant bills, but if you've been happy with the service, it's nice to add a 10% tip.

Toilets
Cretan toilets can't handle toilet paper, which must be deposited in the supplied bin instead. In remote villages, you may still encounter squat toilets.

Tourist Information Offices
Due to budget cuts, there are currently very few regularly staffed tourist offices outside the main summer season.

INDEX

Agia Galini 23
Agia Roumeli 44
Agia Triada 22
Agia Triada, Moni 40
Agios Nikolaos 27–28
Agios Pandeleimon 18
Agios Pavlos 23
Akrotiri Peninsula 39–40
Amari Valley 35–36
Anogia 36–37
Ano Vouves 25
Arkadiou, Moni 34–35
Balos Lagoon 41
Chania 37–39
Chersonissos 24
Chora Sfakion 45
Chrisokalitissa, Moni 41
Chrissi Island 31
Cretaquarium 24
Diktaean Cave 25
Elafonissi 41–42
Elounda 28
Falassarna Beach 41
Fodele 18
Fourfouras 36
Frangokastello 45
Gavdos 42
Gortyn 20–21
Gournes 24
Gournia 29
Gouverneto, Moni 40
Gramvousa Peninsula 41
Ierapetra 31
Imbros Gorge 43, 45
Iraklion 13–17
   Agia Ekaterini 17
   Agios Titos 15
   Archaeological Museum 13–14
   Central Market 17
   City Walls 15
   Historical Museum 17
   Morosini Fountain 17
   Municipal Art Gallery 15–17
   Venetian Harbour 14–15

Imeri Gramvousa 41
Iraklion Wine Country 25
Istro Beaches 28–29
Kalamaki 23
Kalidon 28
Kastelli Kissamou 40–41
Katholiko, Moni 40
Kato Zakros 30–31
Knossos 19–20
Komitades 45
Kommos 23
Kritsa 28
Lendas 21
Loutro 45
Maleme 40
Malia 24–25
Matala 22–23
Minotaur 18
Monastiraki 35
Omalos 44
Paleochora 42
Phaistos 21–22
Plakias 37
Platania 35
Preveli, Moni 37
Preveli Beach 37
Profitis Ilias Hill 39–40
Psiloritis (Mount Ida) 36
Psychro 25
Rethimnon 33–34
Rouvas Gorge 21, 43
Samaria Gorge 42–44
Sideroportes 44
Sirtaki 44
Sitia 29–30
Sougia 42
Spinalonga Island 28
Stavros 40
Sybrita (Syvritos) 35
Thronos 35
Toplou, Moni 25, 30
Triopetra 23
Vaï 30
Vizari 35–36
Zakros Gorge 30, 43
Zaros 21

Editors
Eleonora Di Campli
Birgit Seitz

Concept
Karin Palazzolo

Layout
Luc Malherbe
Matias Jolliet

Photo Credits
P. 1: istockphoto/Domagala
P. 2: fotolia.com/Fabri (oleander), Travel Pictures Ltd (Cretan man); istockphoto.com/Gallas (palace of Knossos); Huber/Huber (beach)

Maps
JPM Publications, Mathieu Germay

Copyright © 2014, 1995
JPM Publications S.A.
12, avenue William-Fraisse,
1006 Lausanne, Suisse
information@jpmguides.com
http://www.jpmguides.com/

All rights reserved. No part of this book may be reproduced or transmitted in any form or by any means, electronic or mechanical, including photocopying, recording or by any information storage and retrieval system without permission in writing from the publisher.

Every care has been taken to verify the information in the guide, but neither the publisher nor his client can accept responsibility for any errors that may have occurred. If you spot an inaccuracy or a serious omission, please let us know.

Printed in Switzerland
15575.00.15515
Edition 2014

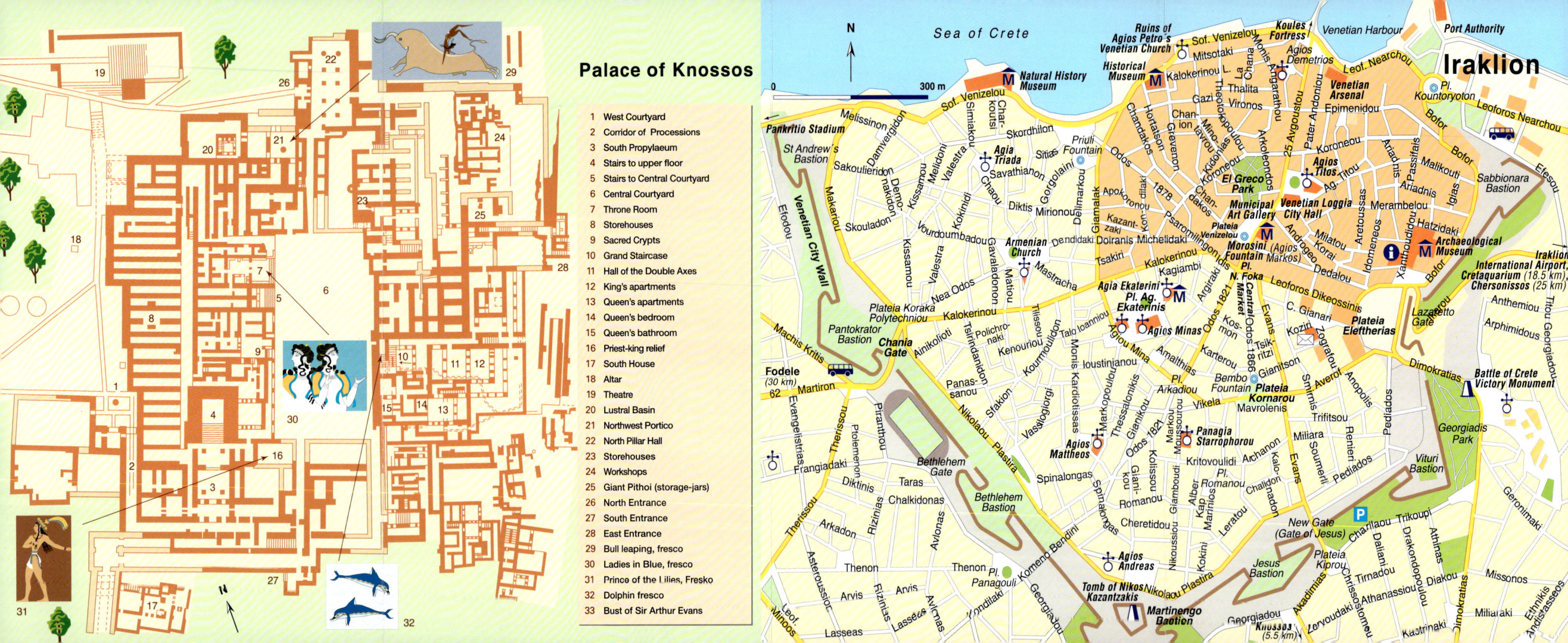